Being an Authorpreneur:
How to Succeed in the Book Business

International Award-Winning Author
Toneal M. Jackson

APS
PUBLISHING

www.weareaps.com

ISBN: 978-0990636137

Table of Contents

Author's Note

The purpose of this book is to provide authors with critical information necessary to succeed in the literary industry. Often time, writers have the mistaken notion that once the book is completed, so is their job; the reality is that it's just the beginning.

In this day and age, many writers opt to use the self-publishing route to get their work to the masses. Whereas this vein does guarantee that your will work be in print, and that your name will be on the front cover, it does not guarantee you fame and/or fortune. Acquiring those will totally depend on how you execute your vision, as both author and entrepreneur.

Once you publish a book, you now have a product for which you are fully responsible – its failure or success lies in your hands. Everything is "do it yourself": marketing, promotion, and sales are all controlled by you. Although that thought may seem a bit overwhelming, by the time you finish reading this book, you should feel better equipped to manage your journey as an authorpreneur.

Learning the Industry

To become educated in the field in which you possess interest.

Writing Conferences

Workshops

Organizations

The number one rule for anyone pursuing any career is to learn the industry. Whether you aspire to be a singer, musician, electrician, cosmetologist, insurance agent, or writer – do yourself a favor, and research what you're about to get yourself into. All too often, individuals see the end results of someone else's work, and assume that the journey must have been easy. They never take the time to find out what it takes to succeed in their respective industry.

Owning your own business requires a lot of time, dedication, perseverance, and yes, money. The old adage, "it takes money to make money" is very true. If you want someone else to invest in you, you must first be willing to invest in yourself.

Writing Conferences

For aspiring authors, attending a writer's conference can be advantageous. It allows the opportunity to meet other individuals in the literary world – authors; agents; editors; even publishers. It also provides an insider's perspective of how the industry operates, including ways to become a published author. Furthermore, it assists in perfecting your personal writing skills by addressing issues you may possess.

Writing conferences are held all over the world, and various times throughout the year. So no matter how hectic your schedule, attending a conference is always a possibility. Listed below are some of the more well-known conferences; by no means does this imply that these are the only conferences or the best to attend, as each targets a different need. This list should be used to get you pointed in the right direction. Keep in mind that most conferences are not free; they all vary in price.

Association of Writers and Writing Programs (AWP) Conference

The largest literary conference in North America, it is geared toward writers, teachers, students, editors and publishers.

Santa Barbara Writers Conference

Connects writers, mentors, agents and editors every summer. Began in 1972.

Writer's Digest Conference

Provides the opportunity to meet, collaborate and network with other writers and industry leaders.

Chicago Writers Conference

Dedicated to connecting local authors and publishing professionals.

Women Writers Conference

Held in Kentucky, this conference hosts women from across the nation to showcase talent of emerging and established authors.

Workshops

Like conferences, writing workshops can help hone your skills as a writer. You can learn things such as how to overcome writer's block; and rules of writing that will assist you in completing your manuscript. Some workshops even teach you how to pitch agents and publishers. Numerous topics can be discussed within the context of a writing workshop, but should allow you to feel more educated and informed about your path once it's over.

Organizations

All types of organizations exist for authors. As with any other organization, their purpose is to provide solidarity; to put a support system in place to prevent the feeling of being alone. The mantra of my organization, Authors Promoting Success, is "We are better together". This communicates to members that not only are they part of something greater than themselves, but those with whom they are affiliated understand their struggle.

Another benefit to joining an organization is the resources it may bring. As a new author, you may not be aware of the various opportunities, events, and expos available. Beyond that, even if you are aware, you may not be able to afford the costs associated with participation. In most cases, belonging to an organization makes participation possible at a much more affordable rate.

Learning from the experience of others is an additional advantage. Instead of having to lose money, or risk being disappointed, you can confer with fellow members and hear their testimonials. Many times, this saves time, money, and heartbreak.

Remember, you have a variety of organizations from which to choose – local or national; those that are gender and/or racially exclusive; some are genre specific; some are just for new authors; and some are solely for indies.

For Chicago natives, besides Authors Promoting Success, which is a national organization that specializes in assisting independent authors gain exposure and achieve success in the literary industry, I would recommend two additional organizations to consider. Chicago Writers Association (of which I have been a member for quite some time), and Chicago Black Authors Network. Both help their members learn more about the industry, and give exposure opportunities locally. With so many options, there's no reason to fight this battle alone.

Writing the Book

Compiling thoughts and ideas into a cohesive format.

Content

Editing

Cover Design

One of the questions I'm asked all the time is, "How do I write a book"? Typically, my reply is, "It depends on what you're writing".

Generally speaking, writing is a process. I don't know many people who say they want to write a book on Monday, and have it completed on Tuesday. Most times, it's because there are so many distractions that life presents – work, spousal and/or parental responsibilities, hobbies – that rarely do you have the chance to just sit and write without interruption. And even if you schedule time to write, you can't make your juices flow. Never has there been a statement so true as "You can't force creativity".

You can write sentence after sentence, but every writer has a point when they can get their "good writing" done; and often time, it's hard to plan for. You can be in the tub, on the train, or at the doctor's office when you get that idea that allows you to write for hours on end. When it happens, you want to stay in that moment until it ends.

Content

It always helps to start with an outline. Regardless of whether you're writing fiction or nonfiction, an outline always proves useful, as it serves as a means to shape your book. It provides the opportunity to determine what you want to discuss in the book.

For nonfiction writers, you can use an outline to breakdown various topics and subtopics, or what should be included within the respective themes. For fiction writers, an outline affords the opportunity to decide what characters and/or scenarios to implement. You can also go into detail about traits and backgrounds for said characters. When done correctly, a complete outline assists in about half of the book writing process.

When writing your first draft (yes, there should be more than one), don't be driven by book order – chapter 1, chapter 2, etc. Your main concern should be getting the content out of your mind and onto the paper; you can spend time "connecting the dots" later. Often time when you write initially, it may not make sense to anyone other than you. If you use a notebook, it may be so many scratch outs that it's embarrassing – just remember, it's all part of the process.

When you rewrite, or what I refer to as the "clean-up" process, you're likely to find words that were left out; written twice; spelled incorrectly; in the wrong order – a variety of mistakes may have been made depending on the conditions and circumstances in which you were writing. The best thing you can do for yourself is get an editor; in fact, it's one of the biggest pieces of advice that I give authors.

Editing

It doesn't matter if you're an English teacher, having an editor never hurts as it provides an extra set of eyes to check your work. First of all, when you write, you tend to lose objectivity because it's *your* work; you think that whatever you print is gospel. Secondly, when you read it, you read what you *think* you wrote as opposed to what's actually on the page. An editor can catch those mistakes and bring them to your attention. Although it can be a costly expense, readers value writers who take the time to produce quality work.

The bigger picture is that this issue usually differentiates an author who self-published from one who used traditional methods. Unfortunately, because everyone who wants to write a book can do so, shortcuts are often taken, which yields an undesirable end product filled with grammatical mistakes and inconsistencies. That's not to say that traditional books are error free, but because the opportunity for review exists, they are a lot less common.

Cover Design

Almost as (if not more) important than the inside of the book is the outside. Ironically enough, the phrase, "Don't judge a book by its cover" does not apply to authors. That's *exactly* what readers use to judge you!

Unless you're a celebrity author who is already established, your cover MUST stand out; otherwise, it will go unnoticed. I can't tell you how many authors I've heard say, "Well, it's a good story". The disappointing fact is that if the cover doesn't compel the reader to pick it up, they will never discover how good the story is.

It may be a good idea to work with a graphic designer and communicate to them not only the book's content, but also your vision for the cover. Many times, if you work with someone skilled in their profession, they may be able to offer some concepts that you may not have thought of that may portray your book better than you could have imagined.

Another common mistake among self-published authors is not putting the synopsis on the back of the book. Being a bookstore owner, I can't tell you how many books are presented to me with a blank back cover. When I ask, "What is your book about?", and the authors begin to reply, my immediate response is, "What happens if a customer wants to know, are you going to be here to tell them"?

It's very arrogant to think that a reader will want to read your book without knowing what it's about. Your cover can be outstanding – enough so that it captivates their attention enough to pick it up. But once they have it in their hand, short of reading through the first chapter or two, how can they know the book's content?

Along with the summary, your back cover should include an "About the Author" section as well. This helps to establish credibility with your readers (which will be addressed in the marketing section of the book). You should also include a headshot to make yourself identifiable.

Getting It Published

Transforming your manuscript into a book
format and producing it for an audience.

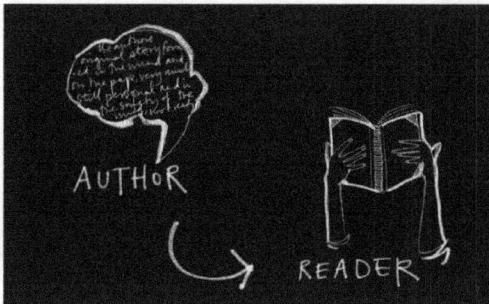

Traditional Houses

Vanity Presses

Print-On-Demand

There are certain characteristics that make a book a book. Regardless of which avenue you employ to bring your book into fruition, some things are not optional. The two I will discuss here are ISBNs and book binding.

Every book should have an ISBN, or International Standard Book Number. This number is what identifies your book across the globe, just as your social security number distinguishes you. Many times, because people don't understand the difference between printing and publishing, they feel that they can eliminate costs by simply going to the nearest Staples or Office Depot and just printing copies of whatever they have written; that is a HUGE no-no in the literary industry. Anyone who has been in this circle for a second, will be able to spot you from afar if you make this tragic mistake.

Unless you plan to solely use what you have produced as registration materials or as a fundraising project, your book MUST have an ISBN, or technically, it is not a book. Not only do most avid readers know the difference, but most companies won't accept it for resale. Again, if you don't plan for your work to be distributed beyond those you know personally, this may resonate well with you. However, if you are among the vast majority of authors who write books so that people can access the information contained inside, then this is a mistake that you definitely DO NOT want to make.

Without an ISBN, your book cannot be: sold online; registered with Amazon or Barnes & Noble (the two largest online book retailers); included in libraries, schools, bookstores, or most other reputable institutions. So although there may be ways to cut corners and scale down on costs, this is not one of them. Remember, just because your material is printed does not mean it is published!

Whether paperback or hardcover, every book should be perfectly bound. Again, an immediate sign of an amateur (and unpublished) writer is having a book bound spirally. That is an immediate sign that your book has not actually been published, rather printed. Every *publishing* institution provides that service to authors. The appearance is more polished and professional. It's not that the content differs from one form of binding to the other, it simply communicates that you are a reputable source because you took the time to get your work produced correctly.

Unless you take the time to acclimate yourself to the industry, it's not something that you may automatically know. So before you publish a book, or even decide with which company you want to align yourself, do some research. Examine a few books – inside and out. Look and see what they all have in common. Compare books from different houses. One of the best signs of professionalism is if you can't distinguish a traditionally published book from a self-published one. Don't know the difference between the two...keep reading.

Traditional Houses

Now that your book is written, you have to get it published, but which road do you take – traditional; self-publishing; or print-on-demand? With so many options, how do you know which is the right one to choose? Well, here's a quick overview of each to help you make an educated decision.

It is very difficult to get signed with traditional publishing houses such as Random House, Simon & Schuster, and McGraw Hill. This is because they usually require you to have a literary agent to represent you. The assumption is that if you have been able to solidify an agent (which is deemed as a reputable source in the industry), then your work must be good, or at least at a level where someone in the industry will vouch for you.

An agent handles the bulk of the work for you, as they are responsible for "shopping" your manuscript around to the various publishing houses since they don't accept unsolicited manuscripts (work unaccompanied by an agent's endorsement). The fact is that most of these houses only accept a few manuscripts a year, which makes it even less likely that yours will be accepted. Many authors tend to give up on this journey after receiving dozens, and even hundreds of rejection letters, as the feeling of defeat becomes overwhelming. However, if your manuscript is selected by a traditional house, you will be extended an offer to sign with them.

This offer usually includes a financial advance (the amount varies with the publishing house), which is the aspect with which most people are familiar. But what may not be understood is that the company is purchasing the rights to your work; so for the duration of the contractual term, you have no say-so as to what goes on with your book.

They design a cover that they feel is the most marketable – regardless of whether it aligns with the vision you may have possessed. If they don't like the content, then you are obligated to change it so that it agrees with what they feel works best. Most times, they schedule appearances for you to help sell the book; although this sounds great, there may be occasions where it conflicts with a personal obligation, and the scheduled event takes precedence.

Overall, as long as you don't mind rejections, and not maintaining creative control over your work, then being published via traditional means may be the way to go. However, if you want to retain power over your work, then self-publishing is for you. There are two different avenues if you choose this route: vanity presses or print-on-demand.

Vanity Presses

Vanity presses such as AuthorHouse, Xlibris, and Dorrance are paid to publish books. So, if you have been rejected or want to maintain creative vision with your project, you may opt to go with one of these companies. The downside to these presses is that you have to pay for every service received. If you send them a manuscript filled with errors, unless you pay them to edit, it will be published exactly how it was received.

This is one of the reasons that self-published authors receive so much criticism and are heavily discriminated against within the literary industry. The perception is that you have no true credibility because you paid to be published. The reality is that many independent authors are just as talented, have messages just as powerful, but simply decided that they didn't want to wait for someone else to deem their work worthy enough to reach the masses.

In the same vein of these companies is

America Star Books (formerly Publish America) who classify themselves as a traditional publisher because they issue no upfront costs. They even claim to offer their authors an advance, which is 1¢...that's right, they issue a check in the amount of one cent! If you were to compare them with vanity presses, the advantage is that you don't have to pay them to publish your book; however, the fees they assess to buy your book are astronomically high. They typically charge a minimum of $12 per book; so it would cost $120 to buy 10 books – and that doesn't include shipping and taxes!

So as an entrepreneur, what that means to you is that you'd have to price your book at a minimum of $15 just to break even...not make a profit, just to recoup your expenses. Now if you have a 200-page novel, that may sound reasonable, but it's unfathomable for an author of a 30 page children's book! Although it may appear financially appealing initially (because upfront publishing fees are eliminated), they make up for it in the end when you purchase your books – unless you're not looking to buy a substantial amount.

Print-On-Demand

Companies such as CreateSpace, Lulu, and Book Baby provide the opportunity to do all of the work yourself. Beyond the writing, you can upload your complete manuscript, which includes the formatted interior and book cover (CreateSpace even has a template that assists in cover creation). Also included in this process is pricing your book, and even publishing it as a paperback and/or e-book on Amazon.

This is an excellent outlet for creative individuals who understand the process – or at the very least, don't mind taking the time to learn how to execute it. In many cases, it is this reason that people don't choose this option...they don't have the time or patience to effectively master this method.

The benefit is that you don't have to pay any publishing costs (other than editing and cover design); and the fee to purchase your book is very nominal so making a profit is very realistic. The best advantage is that you don't have to worry about wasting inventory; as the name suggests, you only have to have your books printed when you need them.

My imprint, APS Publishing, combines characteristics from all of these companies: it provides a reputable logo and editing services like a traditional house; allows you to maintain creative control like a vanity press; and affords the ability to only order books when you need them like a print-on-demand. Even though our rates are extremely reasonable, we offer payment plans. Perhaps the best part, is that you are able to work with an International Award-Winning Author – someone who has gone through the process, and is capable to provide guidance and serve as a mentor throughout your journey!

Marketing

To advertise; to make others aware of your product/service in efforts to encourage purchase, use or endorsement.

NEW!

Establish Credibility

Social Media

Websites

Establish Credibility

Many authors underestimate the importance of establishing credibility – in other words, why should readers purchase your book? With so many books on the market, what makes your book unique? The answer to these questions can usually be found in either the synopsis or the "about the author" sections of the book.

If placed on the back cover, your credibility can be established using reviews from prominent individuals – either within the industry in which you're writing, or a well-known public figure who is respected by the general population. For example, if you're writing a children's book, and Judy Blume had a positive critique, placing her comments on the back cover is perceived as an endorsement. If someone already well-known for doing what you do says that it's good, then others may purchase it just because of their approval.

Or, if you happen to know a celebrity (regardless of topic connection) who will either write something positive, or take a picture with your book, you can benefit from their clout. I've had the good fortune of having Eriq LaSalle, Kym Whitley, and Nick Cannon to take pictures with my books.

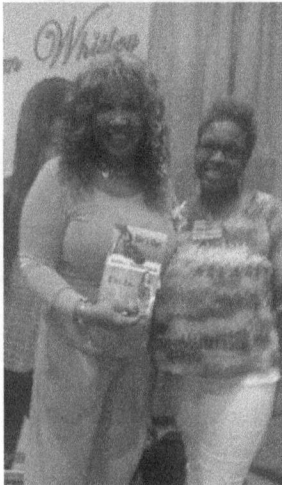

Isaiah Washington not only took a picture with me and my book, but he also tweeted about it! So now, when I go to sell those books, others are motivated to purchase them because they know that, if nothing else, the aforementioned celebrities also have them.

Another way of establishing credibility is by sharing your personal credentials. For example, if you're writing a book on ministry and are a licensed evangelist or pastor, or have a degree in theology, it's beneficial to tell your readers as they may trust your content a little more. Or maybe, like one of my clients, you are a beauty maven who decides to write a book on the topic. You can share your practical and professional experiences and expertise with others. So in short, any educational, practical, or industrial experience should be highlighted to distinguish you from everyone else.

Establishing credibility also occurs upon winning contests. But, in order to win a contest, you must first apply. This implies that you have monies reserved (which will be covered later in the section on book budgets).

While every contest does not require that you pay an entry fee, many do. Most times, you are mandated to send a physical copy of your book to the judges. No two contests are alike; each has their own criteria regarding fees, rules and guidelines. Also, be aware that you are not the only one who knows about these contests. Usually, your book will be one of hundreds, if not thousands being reviewed.

The contest for the National Black Book Festival does not require a fee; however, it is only for new authors. I was fortunate to rank #3 as their best new author in 2011.

To qualify for the Newberry Award, you must be the author of a children's book written the year prior to entry. For example, if you desire to enter your book for consideration of a 2016 award, it has to have been published in 2015. There is no fee for this contest.

Then, there is the Readers' Favorite International Book Awards. This contest is so special because entrants come from all over the world; so competition for this contest is very fierce. My book, Inspiration from A.B.O.V.E., received the Silver Medal in the Inspirational category in 2013.

The list of book contests goes on and on, as

there are hundreds of them. Just like with anything else, you want to do your research. Check the website; contact previous winners; you want to ensure that anything requesting payment is legitimate.

What's the purpose of going through all of the rigmarole, you ask? Although there are slim chances that you will win, IF you win, you are now known as "Award-Winning Author" your name here. In many cases, people are more likely to pick up an award-winning book – even though the content is still the same – it is now perceived to be better.

Being a bestselling author is in the same realm as being an award-winning one. The difference is that possessing this title is based solely upon the number of books you sell in a specified period of time. To be considered bestselling on Amazon, you need to sell around 3000-5000 books in 24 hours. Even if you don't sustain your position, you will always be able to retain your title. In other words, if you sell a certain amount of books one time, you will forever be referred to be as a "Bestselling" Author.

Social Media

Facebook. Twitter. LinkedIn. Pinterest. Instagram. What do these all have in common? They are among the most popular websites for social media. Although people still use telephones, more likely than not, they are using them to post, tweet, or upload a picture or video. What's my point? The way people communicate and the methods they employ are constantly changing.

As an authorpreneur, it is your job to be current with these trends. Don't get me wrong, I'm not saying that you have to have an account on every site listed, but you should have at least one. To know which is the most beneficial for you, you must first know the purpose of each.

Facebook, the most popular social media site, receives almost one BILLION views a month! Whether or not you choose to have a personal page is optional, but you should definitely create a fan page. The purpose of this is to inform your Facebook friends of your status as an author. So it would probably be a good idea to use a picture of yourself as the profile picture, and a picture of your book (or any product that you desire to sell or create awareness), as your cover picture. Some choose to use the most current book as the profile picture so that whenever you post (write a message), people will see that picture. Subliminally, they are receiving the message to purchase that book – or at least inquire about it.

If you are consistent with your posting, it is simple to build a fan base, which can in turn become buyers of your product. It's not difficult to do, and is a free means of advertisement (unless you choose to pay for promotion); the only thing it costs is your time. If it's starting to feel a bit overwhelming, remember that it's always possible to organize your day to allow for posting.

Make your messages brief – write something in route to work (if you're not driving); or on your lunch break and/or before you go to bed. Just make sure they are purposeful; can help someone; and keeps your audience updated on your whereabouts: upcoming events, projects, etc. Most importantly, make sure that your posts are consistent with your brand messaging; if you are a Christian author, you shouldn't be using profanity!

Twitter has over three million monthly views. One of the main differences between the two social media platforms is the permitted message length; Facebook is unlimited, and Twitter is 140 characters (words, punctuation, everything combined cannot exceed this limit). While it may appear challenging to master your messages with 140 characters or less, the Twittersphere is the perfect place to blast (tweet) a quick message. You can personalize those tweets to not only people that follow you, but anyone whose handle (twitter profile name) that you know.

I remember once I tweeted something about Donnie McClurkin's voice while watching the BET Gospel Awards, and BET retweeted it! Or, in Facebook lingo, they shared my post with all of their friends. Point being that you never know who may find interest in your tweets and take the time to help spread your message.

LinkedIn has over a quarter billion views every month. This site is typically more business oriented, where Facebook is more social in nature. Depending on the type of book you write – especially if it can be used in a corporate setting, becoming acclimated with this site can be advantageous.

Although Pinterest is a more popular site than Instagram, they pretty much function the same. They allow you the opportunity to use pictures to convey your message. For example, if your book is about to be published, you can use the front cover and "pin" it (post for viewers to see) or upload it to Instagram with the caption possibly being the release date.

It may sound like a lot to do – that's because it is. Becoming a household name isn't easy, and won't happen overnight. It is a process that will take a lot of your time, patience, dedication, and money. But that's why you want to have a business plan in place before you get started. You want to have realistic goals, and a means of accomplishing them. Your books won't sell on their own, and unless you already have billions of dollars and teams of people in place to do it for you – be prepared to invest a lot of blood, sweat, and tears along the way.

Even though there are many forms of marketing that do cost, for the most part, using social media is free, and can be extremely rewarding. Keep in mind that social media is worldwide, so gone are the days of limited reach. Your book can reach someone on any of the seven continents – so becoming an international author is not as difficult as it may sound. It does take work, but it is possible.

Websites

Hand in hand with a social media presence is possessing a personal website. Why is it necessary, you ask? Many feel if they have a Facebook page that having their own website is optional and/or extra work. But the truth is that you don't *own* your Facebook page; if the creators decided to shut the site down tomorrow, all of your pictures and posts would be gone forever. For this reason (and others), it is best to have your own website.

Yes, you can use it in conjunction with social media. You can post on your preferred sites and refer readers back to your website, if you choose. But ultimately, the reason why a website is important is because it too adds credibility. Think of your website as the home address for your book (or whatever product you sell).

It's great to post on social media, but you're only as relevant as your last interaction. Go an hour without posting, and literally, a thousand others have replaced you in the newsfeed. Your website is dedicated solely to you, your message, and your product. Your supporters, fans, followers, etc. can have a consistent medium to stay connected.

You may say, "My books are on Amazon, so can't I just send interested parties there?" Well, sure you can if you don't mind giving away about 60-70% of your royalties. Amazon is great at what they do. They are a global distribution company, so their job is simply to display your product thereby giving you an opportunity for global visibility. Although there may not be an upfront cost for this service, you will pay.

As an example, if you have a book that lists for $14.99, depending on the deal you have, you may only receive $4-$5, which if you did the math is only about 30%. The rest is used to order and ship your book and pay Amazon. But, if you had your own website to refer those you know to visit, the only cost you'd incur is the 3% that PayPal charges and shipping (if you opt to assume that cost). So you receive a bigger piece of the pie.

But don't get me wrong, I am not insinuating that you should avoid an Amazon affiliation because remember, they are a GLOBAL company. And unless you personally know people all over the world, they have a far greater reach than you. What I am suggesting is that you use all of the mediums together for your benefit. Use social networks + Amazon + your personal website to yield the best results.

And, having a website in and of itself is another means of adding credibility. For example, if you interact with someone and they genuinely like your presentation, but just may not be equipped to support you financially, it doesn't have to be a lost opportunity. Instead, you can simply refer them to your website where they can support you at a later time.

Contrary to popular belief, websites are not only for rich people. Many free websites exist such as weebly.com and webs.com that allow you to design your site for free. If you want to really look professional, you can go to a hosting site like godaddy.com or ehost.com to secure a domain name for your site. So instead of icecream.weebly.com, by paying for hosting, you can eliminate the suffix and simply be known as icecream.com. Hosting is very inexpensive; depending on the site you use, it can be as little as $12 a year.

The most expensive cost associated with having a website is designing it. If you don't know how, and don't want to and/or don't have the time to learn (which can be done by watching YouTube tutorials), then you will have to pay someone to do it for you. Again, I would caution you to do research or ask for referrals before agreeing to do business with the first person to provide a quote. Prices can start in the hundreds and go into the thousands. As with anything else, feel free to ask for samples of the person's work to ensure that you like the quality. After all, this is a subjective process – everyone's costs and tastes vary.

Promotions

Advertisements; methods of informing the public about your product/service.

Read any good books lately?

How and when to do them

Book Budgets

Reviews

How and When

When writing a book, there are different ways and times in which you can promote it. Some authors use a three-to-six-month advance notice window to make their book available on pre-order. In other words, they have an idea of when the book will be released, so they take advantage of that time frame to pique the interest of their supporters. During this time, you are notifying family, friends, co-workers, neighbors, church and community members, people on social media, etc. that you have a book coming out and that you would appreciate their support in this endeavor.

Allowing your book to be pre-ordered is a special incentive for those to show advance support. Typically, the price is discounted, or includes an autograph, picture – something that those who order it after the release would not receive. You want to encourage individuals to support you and build a fan base.

Another promotion that authors use is a

book giveaway. Whether or not you do it before the official release is up to you; the purpose is to gather information from your readers to help grow your fan base. I'll repeat it over and over, the entire purpose of marketing and promotion is to grow your fan base. Whether the methods you employ are free or paid, their purpose should be to make others aware of you and your product.

This is the purpose of the book giveaway. Yes, it may cost money to buy (and ship) the book. However, if the recipient can help bring attention your way – help spread the word – then in the long run, it's worth it. Whether they post a review on Amazon, Barnes & Noble, Goodreads, or a social media network, someone that didn't know about you before now does. Word of mouth still proves to be the most effective source of advertisement. You never know who knows who; by reaching out to one person, you're ultimately touching many.

I can't begin to tell you how many more of my books sold once people knew that a celebrity read my book. Or how many people wanted to buy one once it garnered an award. Or how my sales increased after a Facebook discussion – or a fan posted a picture holding my book. These are all proven tactics that work!

I'll never forget when I met Isaiah Washington and he got a copy of my book.

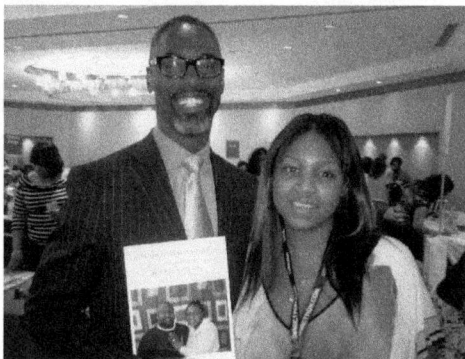

When I asked if he'd take a picture with me, his response was, "Yes – let's get some of these books sold!" He understood the power of effective promotion – how he could use his celebrity to positively affect sales.

Another opportunity to implement a promotion is during holidays. It's always a great idea to discount your book for Mother's Day, Christmas, or any holiday that pertains to your book. For example, if your book is about love or relationships, you may want to highly promote it around Valentine's or Sweetest Day. Got a book about the military? Then Veteran's Day or Memorial Day may be an opportune time to run your promotion. Some authors even incorporate the release of their book in this manner to help build even more momentum. It's a plethora of ways to let the world know about your book.

But before you implement these promotions, you should have your book budget in place. What is a book budget, you ask? Continue reading to find out!

Book Budgets

A book budget refers to the monies needed to effectively execute your business plan. Just as a household incorporates a home's expenses, a book budget includes all things associated with an author's expense. While every budget may vary, as the amount depends on income, efficient planning should ensure your ability to partake in at least (3) of the following (7) items:

- Book Orders
- Events
- Contests
- Promo Materials (business cards/book marks/flyers/posters)
- Marketing
- Website
- Merchandise (t-shirts; hats; etc.)

There are no "right" or "wrong" pieces to this puzzle as they all work together to build your brand. However, I would definitely make sure that monies are set aside for book orders. Many times authors agree to doing an event without taking inventory of how many books they have on hand. Not having a sufficient amount of books doesn't allow you to maximize your opportunity financially, and may ultimately make attending the event no longer worthwhile.

My Preferred Order:
1. **Book orders**
2. **Website** (*An author's online residence*)
3. **Events** (*Gives people an opportunity to put a name to the face*)
4. **Marketing** (*Helps spread the word about who you are; what you do; how people can support you - buy a book; like a page; attend an event*)
5. **Promo Materials** (*A keepsake that reminds its recipients who you are*)
6. **Contests** (*Adds credibility*)
7. **Merchandise** (*Strengthens the brand; another way to convey the same message*)

If I had to pick (2) that could be omitted from the budget for a novice author, it would be contests and merchandise. It's not because these items are not important, but because they give a boost to an existing brand. The other pieces are essential to initially building and establishing one's brand.

So evaluate where you are in this journey. If you're just starting out, then investing in a website and events are critical to your success as an author. On the other hand, if you've been out for a while (a year or more), and only have one book, it may be a good idea to invest in contests and merchandise as a means of reinventing yourself.

However, the first step is to determine how much you are willing to invest in yourself, and your business...after all, you are an AUTHORPRENEUR, and as with anything, you get out of it, what you put into it!!!

Reviews

Earlier in this section, I spoke of giving a book away in order to receive a review in exchange. The reason why authors believe in this process is because it helps establish credibility. There are other ways to receive reviews. You can ask people to leave a review once they've purchased your book. There are websites such as ReadersFavorite.com that provide free book reviews. You can also ask a blogger to review your book.

The purpose the book review serves is really to notify the public what people are saying about your book. For better or worse, what others think can play a critical role to your success. Think about it, how many times do you allow knowing how many stars a movie received to alter your decision as to whether or not to go see it? Or, if a friend gave a restaurant terrible reviews, you avoid it? It happens all the time; however, it's not to say that you won't be able to sell any books without reviews. You will just have to be more effective in your sales strategies and techniques.

Sales

The monies acquired as a result of selling your product.

Accepting payments

Live Events

Online

This portion of the book is perhaps the part that most are excited to read because everyone wants to know or hear about making money. After all, that's the reason you became an author isn't it (or at least one of them)? Now that you've educated yourself about the literary industry; written the book; and done some marketing and promotion, it's time to make some money.

You want to be prepared to accept all forms of payment; remember, we are living in a day and age where very few people carry cash. Think about it, the last time you made a purchase, how did you pay for it? Nine times out of ten, you used a debit/credit card; your customers will be no different.

The last thing you want to do after working so hard to pique that customer's interest is to lose them because you don't accept card payments. Do yourself a favor and order a device that allows you to do so.

Accepting Payments

It used to be a time where if you wanted to accept credit cards, you had to lug around a huge credit card machine. You could only use it if you had access to electricity; and you had to pay a monthly service fee whether you used it or not. But nowadays, there are so many portable options; they only require attachment to a smartphone or tablet, and only assess a fee when used.

Of all the devices, PayPal Here; Intuit; Pay Anywhere; Square may be the most popular. Regardless of which you use, all are free to order (unless you buy it in a retail store); so there are no reasons to have to turn away a potential sale. You want your customers to make their purchase when they're in your presence, because although they may have the best of intentions, once they leave, the likelihood of them remembering to go home to buy your book are not great.

Additionally, if you are an exhibitor/vendor, you want to be certain to bring change with you. Always have at least 20 singles because you don't know what denomination (bill) the customer may desire to use. If your book sells for $10, and they have a $20 bill, you want to be able to give them proper change – not encourage them to find change and come back. You want to make the process of their purchase as simple as possible.

Typically, as a rule of thumb, I don't accept personal checks unless I actually know the person – I've called them; been to their house; know their family; etc. I have found that people can seem as sweet as pie, but once you accept that check and give them your merchandise, if it doesn't clear, it's going to take a lot to get your money back (sometimes you end up eating the costs). If it's an entity such as a church, school, or business, then that's a different matter. Usually those checks will clear without any issues. But again, the forms of payment that you accept is at your discretion.

At the end of the day, this is business, and you should run it as such. One of your principal reasons of becoming an entrepreneur is to make money. If you go through all of the work to get to this stage, you want to be prepared to reap the benefits.

Book Events: Live

A book event refers to any opportunity an author has to sell books and/or network. These events can be held locally or nationally. Local events typically refer to events held within one's immediate place of residency, while national refers to places abroad. However, for my intents and purposes, local events will refer to those with an attendance of less than 100 people; while national will refer to those with more than 1000.

There are many different kinds of venues that host live events – schools; libraries; book clubs; and expos – just to name a few. If you are the type of author that prefers a more intimate setting, with smaller crowds (whether it's because you're introverted or because you want to get to know your fans), you may opt to do book talks at libraries, book clubs or churches.

Typically, this environment lends itself to no more than 30-40 people who are eager to hear what you have to say about your journey. "What made you want to become an author?" "How did you come up with the title for your book?" "Are you working on another book?" These are common questions that you will find yourself addressing because you are the main attraction.

Schools

With school literary events and expos, it can be more impersonal. You're really just trying to sell as many books as possible. You are one of many vendors (there are sometimes hundreds or even thousands), and don't have the time to monopolize the attention of the attendees. You have a few seconds – maybe two minutes to make a lasting impression. The benefit of these events is that, if executed properly, you can move a hefty amount of merchandise in a short amount of time.

Be aware that in order to do business with most schools, you must have a vendor license, or some contractual agreement that allows you to do business with them. Every school is different, so if you have a book that has a scholastic theme – bullying; sharing; writing (anything that teaches a lesson) –

you may want to take the steps necessary to initiate a partnership. Be prepared to make pitches, explaining not only the concept of your book, but how it can help the students. Remember, in order to solidify most deals, people want to know how they can benefit from your product/service. The partnership probably will not be formed overnight; it may take a series of conference calls and face-to-face meetings, but once it does happen, it will prove to be well worth the effort.

Libraries

Most libraries sponsor various literary events; many times the focus is to provide an opportunity to connect readers with authors. So once your book is published and printed, it's a good idea to introduce yourself to the branch manager and librarian; leave a complimentary copy of your book for review. So the next time they host a local author book fair or meet & greet, yours may be among the first names on their list to invite.

Book Clubs

Getting connected to a book club can be a

little tricky. This is because many book clubs read books from a particular author or have a preferred genre; so if you write outside of their guidelines, you may not be considered. Then some book clubs may express interest, but it may be awhile before they contact you because they may only read one book a month, and they already have several selections waiting.

However, receiving an opportunity to present to a book club is awesome because they typically ensure that every member purchases a copy of your book. And, if you are the author of multiple titles, you could potentially have a great night. On top of that, book club members are loyal and avid readers who will not only provide you with an online review, but will also refer you to others.

Expos

When it comes to cost, most of the smaller, locally based events have a very nominal fee, if any at all; however, you don't know how many people, if any, will attend. If you decide to participate in a national expo like The Black Women's Expo; Indiana Black

Expo; The Ultimate Women's Expo, just to name a few, be prepared to spend hundreds, and even thousands of dollars to participate. If you happen to be a member of an organization, it generally affords you the opportunity to participate on some level, and the fee is feasible.

The reason the cost is so extravagant for these events is because the reward is usually great. You're exposed to thousands of people, and typically includes various forms of media (television, radio and newspapers). You have the opportunity to meet people from across the country, and get exposure for your work that you wouldn't ordinarily receive.

The factors that I consider when considering whether to participate in any event are:

- How much does the total event cost (travel; food; hotel; parking, etc.)?
- How many hours (days) is the event?
- Are there any additional opportunities (external/intangible, i.e. media interviews; speaking engagements)?

Here's the equation I apply to determine my decision:

$$\text{Hours per day / total cost + benefits} = \text{my time}$$

So if the event costs $300 (and no other associated expenses exist), and it lasts 3 days, that means that I have to make at least $100 a day to break even. This information helps determine the amount to price my books for that event (if you don't have the option to adjust your price, then just factor the cost of your book as it stands). If I sell my book for $10, that means that I would have to sell 10 books a day to make $100, and if the event is 10 hours a day, I'd have to average selling one book an hour. For me, that's something I know I could easily execute (and exceed), which means that without considering any other factors, this event will be profitable.

Now, if the event either costs more, or there are extra expenses associated, or the event lasts a shorter period of time, then the amount of money needed to break even increases. Your goal should be to at least break even, and the external/intangible benefits can make up the difference. No two people are the same, so your determining factors may vary, which is perfectly fine.

The bottom line is that there are tons of exposure opportunities, but you must have a plan as to which ones make sense for you. For example, you may participate in an event because of the location; other participants; platform; or the exposure, regardless of the return on investment.

For you, it may be worth paying $1000 to attend an event in which you only make $100. Some may agree with your decision feeling it depends on the type of event. If there is a chance to meet celebrities, or network with the "right" individuals, then the monies used can be perceived as an investment; others may disagree because they don't want to lose $900. Only you know your budget, goals, and overall blueprint of literary expectations. You have to make the decision that works best for you.

Online

So maybe you've decided that you're not a lover of live events and mingling with the public. Or perhaps, your book budget won't allow you to attend costly events. Is there still a way for you to be successful? Of course.

With the advent of social media, there are a plethora of ways to interact with your fan base. You can create a group on Facebook in which you discuss the content of your book. If you're a novelist, you can discuss characters; if you're a nonfiction writer, you can provide daily tips to create discussion. The more interactive you are, the more you establish yourself as an expert, the more likely people are to want to know more about what you have to say. Thus, the easier it becomes to send them to Amazon or your website to purchase your products. *This same concept can be applied to Twitter, LinkedIn, Pinterest, Instagram, and any other social media platform.*

Another way to gain exposure online is to

write (or guest post) blogs. Blogs are discussions about a particular topic that are meant to be informal and conversational in nature. So, it would be similar to what you would write in a Facebook group, but you'd typically post it on your website to draw more attention to your personal message(s). When you write for someone else's blog, the benefit is that you get exposed to their audience, which could potentially turn into more readers/fans for you.

You can also do online interviews as a way to grow your fan base. Whether on Skype, radio, or Twitter parties, any platform that grants the opportunity for exposure is great. All of these avenues can introduce you to individuals that may be interested in what you have to say, which may lead to another book sale. Remember, nothing is guaranteed, so you have to always create an opportunity to allow yourself to succeed.

Knowing Your Rights

Being educated on the benefits you will, or should accumulate as an entrepreneur.

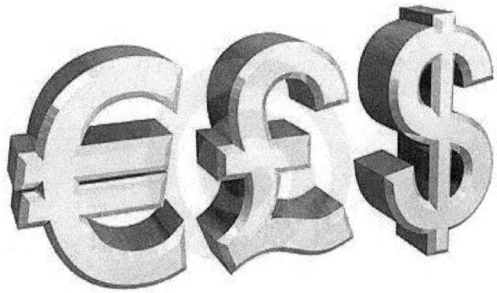

Copyrights

Royalties

Taxes

Some individuals endeavor to be entrepreneurs because they feel that it is an easy meal ticket; they feel that it doesn't or won't take much to make a quick buck. Once the product is created, produced, or published, the idea is to just sell it as quickly as possible for as much as possible. As long as the outcome is only anticipated to be a short-term project, or something that can help get from point A to point B, I guess the thought is, "why bother taking the steps to ensure that the business is legitimate"?

"It takes so much money and time obtaining copyright; getting licensed; incorporated; opening a business account; etc." That's very true – taking the steps to be considered a reputable company aren't easy, but they are necessary. You want to protect yourself from any problems or liabilities that may arise in the future. If you're thinking, "None of those things will ever be an issue for me", my reply is simple: "Nothing is ever a problem until it is".

Copyright

Every author should acclimate themselves with copyright. Copyright is "the exclusive legal right to reproduce, publish, sell, or distribute the matter and form of something (as a literary, musical or artistic work)". This means that if you can possess legal ownership of your work, no one can use it without your permission; if they do, you have the legal right to sue them.

What happens if you avoid paying the fee to get your work copy written? Does it still belong to you? Technically, yes. However, if a situation arises where someone uses your work (or parts of it), you must be able to prove that you were the original owner; and that may not be easy to do without legal documentation.

The simplest thing to do to save yourself money, time, and tears in the long run, is to go www.copyright.gov and register your copyright. It only costs $35. Although it can take up to 13 months to receive your document, you legally possess ownership of the copyright upon uploading your manuscript, filling out the paperwork, and paying the fee. Completing this process ensures that if you ever find that someone has used your work, for any reason, without your permission, you can take legal recourse.

Royalties

A royalty payment is a percentage of the money you receive as a result of selling your book. If you self-publish, you would receive your royalties from online sources such as CreateSpace, Amazon Kindle, or Lulu directly. It is always helpful to remember that a royalty is not the same as the amount in which the book retails. For example, if your book sells for $12.99 online, you will not receive that amount for each unit sold. What you will receive is a small portion, possibly 30% (close to $4.00) for each.

The source from which your book is purchased and the amount of books sold determine the amount of your royalty. If you publish via CreateSpace, you get a certain amount if readers buy your book from the Amazon site; another amount if they buy it directly from CreateSpace; and an entirely different amount if purchased from a third party online retailer.

The offers from brick and mortar stores may vary altogether. At one bookstore, I was offered 60% commission; another only offered 40%. Keep in mind that although you may not be able to control a store's policies, you can decide whether it's beneficial for you. Like with anything else, you want to make sure that whatever moves you make align themselves with your particular business plan.

If you sign with a traditional publisher, you are bound by the terms of your contract. For the most part, you will not receive any royalties until after the publisher has earned its advance payment back from the book sales. Once they recoup those fees, you still only receive a certain percentage of sales until a certain amount of books have sold. As an example, you may only receive 10% of sales for 100,000 books; after that, your percentage may increase. But again, every publisher offers something different, so you want to be sure to read your contract carefully before signing the dotted line.

Whether traditionally or self-published, royalties are received either quarterly or bi-annually (every six months). This is important to note, as most authors feel that they will be rich upon receiving their royalty payment. Especially for self-publishers, a.k.a. do-it-yourselfers, understand that unless you are campaigning heavily, or have a team constantly working for you driving traffic to your book, you will not retire from the royalties you receive.

But I don't want to make it sound depressing because the fact is that there is money to be made from being an author. It is possible to make hundreds of dollars a month (the great authors make thousands) in royalties. It's just like anything else – you get out it what you put into it. If you only promote your book sometime, you'll only get paid sometime. If you treat it as a job, and show loyalty and dedication, putting in consistent work, then you'll reap those benefits as well.

Taxes

Perhaps the easiest thing to overlook, or forget about, when it comes to writing is paying taxes. Remember, this is a business so you must treat it as such. If you have received royalty payments (which will be sent by your publisher if you used traditional methods, or Amazon if you self-published via CreateSpace or Kindle), you must report them on your taxes.

Whether you file as a sole proprietor, or are incorporated, you must report to the IRS the monies you have received for the year. This report is not just limited to your royalty payments, but any monies you received that were associated with the sale of your book. So if you attended book expos or events, those monies should be reported.

You should also keep a record of the monies spent to participate in said events. If you paid to be a vendor, keep track of how much you paid; this includes parking, travel expenses, hotel accommodations, food, etc. All of these expenses must be documented.

Depending on how you file, and or how well you did for the year, it can really prove to be a profitable business.

Conclusion

It takes a lot of work to be successful as an author – or an entrepreneur of any kind for that matter. However, if you prepare yourself, the road won't appear as difficult. That's not to say that being prepared will eliminate heartache and tears altogether, but it is to say that preparation and organization will help to eliminate some.

If you are an aspiring author, you want to get your manuscript published and go to the next level, then my advice to you is to do it. Don't keep waiting, or psyching yourself out saying that you'll get it done next week, next month, or next year because you'll never get it done. Hold yourself accountable for taking that next step.

If you've already submitted your manuscript to a publisher, or are awaiting your finished product, then start working on building your fan base. Work the connections you've already established – your family, friends, co-workers, church members – ask everyone you know to help support you by purchasing a book. When they see how enthusiastic you are about your accomplishment, most (probably not all) will be happy for you. You'll find that not only will they buy a book, but they'll encourage their network of friends to do the same!

If your book is already published, and you're not seeing your desired results, I encourage you to go back and reevaluate your business plan. What things are not happening the way you anticipated? Was your initial goal unrealistic? If so, feel free to change it.

The fact is that sometimes when we write a plan without the actual experience, our perception of what we think we should be able to do isn't realistic. Most times it takes receiving that "on-the-job-training" to know how to truly measure your results. Perhaps, you forgot the standard you set for yourself. If so, again feel free to create another one. That's why we write in pencil – nothing ever has to be permanent!

Even your personal definition of success

may change, and that's perfectly fine.
Remember, the only person that you must
prove yourself to is yourself. If selling one
book a month meets your goal, then once
you do that, you are successful. If you could
care less about making money, and just
want to reach someone with your message
to help them avoid mistakes you made, if
you do that, then you are successful.

Being a successful authorpreneur does not
have one concrete look. For some, it may be
measured by the number of books sold; for
others it may be based upon the amount of
awards received; others may measure it
according to how many people they affected
in a positive way. All I can say is that you'll
know it when you get there!

Other Books by Toneal M. Jackson

Pleasing Your Partner: A Spiritual Guide to
H.A.P.P.I.N.E.S.S.

She's Out. I'm In. Solutions to 7
Relationship Problems

It's A Way to Say It All: How to
Communicate with Your Partner

It's A Way to Say It All: How to
Communicate with Your Kids

Growing Up to Be Happy

Learning to Love Me: Ordinary Women with
Extraordinary Stories

Inspiration from A.B.O.V.E.

Four Girls: A Lot of Choices

Four Girls Learn their Colors

Journals by Toneal M. Jackson

Being an Authorpreneur:
The Entrepreneur's Journal

Writing Journals:
Growing Up to be Happy

Four Girls:
Autumn
Areana
Angele
Jeriah

Reflection Journals:
Inspiration from A.B.O.V.E.

Too Much of a Sinner

Love Me Please

When Love is Just a One-Way Street

Things I Wish I Had the Chance to Say

Learning to Love Me:
Creative Writing Journal

Interested in having your book published?

Contact APS Publishing

Accepts fiction, nonfiction, poetry,
inspirational and children's genres

(855) WER – 1APS or (855) 937-1277

In the Chicagoland area?

Visit **APS Books & More Bookstore**
7601 S. Cicero
Chicago, IL 60652

www.weareaps.com

apsnternational@gmail.com

CPSIA information can be obtained
at www.ICGtesting.com
Printed in the USA
LVHW082207020322
712223LV00017B/1949